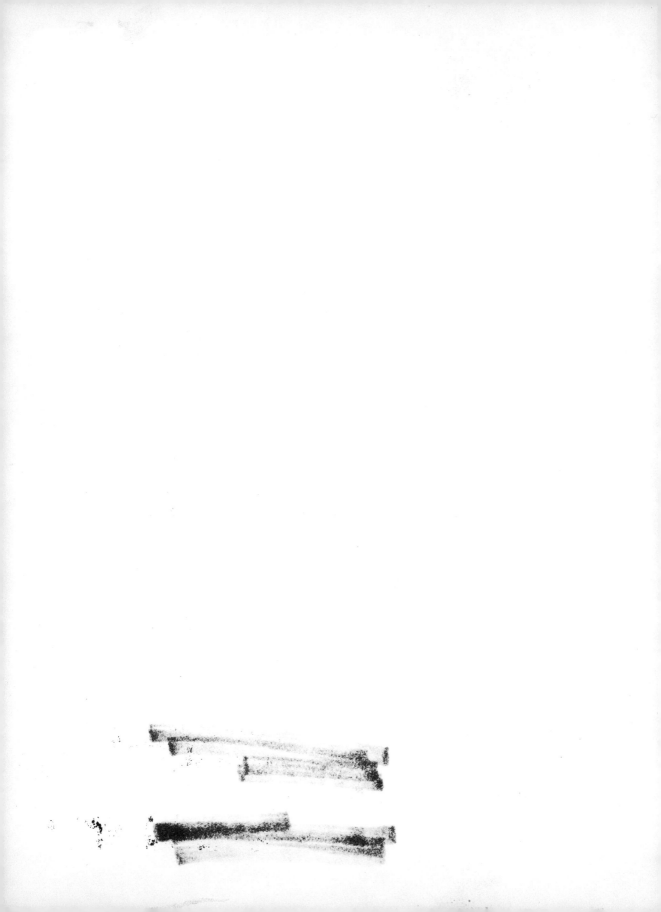

OUR Easter BOOK

by Jane Belk Moncure
illustrated by Lois Axeman

THE
CHILD'S
WORLD

ELGIN, ILLINOIS 60120

Distributed by Childrens Press, 1224 West Van Buren Street, Chicago, Illinois 60607.

Library of Congress Cataloging in Publication Data

Moncure, Jane Belk.
  Our Easter book.

  (A Special-day book)
  Summary: Describes various classroom activities in preparation for Easter.
  1. Easter—Juvenile literature.   2. Schools—Exercises and recreations—Juvenile literature.   [1. Easter]
I. Axeman, Lois, ill.   II. Title.   III. Series.
GT4935.M57   1987   394.2'68283   86-29876
ISBN 0-89565-345-1

2 3 4 5 6 7 8 9 10 11 12 R 96 95 94 93 92 91 90 89

283

OUR Easter BOOK

This book is about things we did at Easter time in our class. You will have many more ideas in your class.

"I saw a robin on my way to school today," said Jeff.

"Seeing robins is a sure sign of spring," said Miss Huff. "Can you think of other signs of spring?"

"Flowers," said Pam.

"Birds making nests," said Billy.

"Trees getting leaves," Eddie said.

"Let's fill our bulletin board with pictures that show signs of spring," said Miss Huff.

Jamie drew Easter lilies. Billy drew a kite. Pam drew an Easter bunny.

"I have a real bunny at home," Pam said.

"Maybe he can visit our room," said Miss Huff.

The next day, Pam brought her bunny
to school. "His name is Nabbit," she said.

Everyone liked Nabbit.

Spring Easter Garden for Nabbit the Rabbit

lettuce

beans

cabbage

radishes

tomatoes

When we made a big vegetable garden behind Nabbit's cage, Eddie said, "With all these vegetables, Nabbit should feel right at home."

"Read us the story about Peter Rabbit," Billy said.

So Miss Huff did. Then we made books about rabbits. And we made bunny puppets out of paper bags.

I had a little 🐇 rabbit.
I put him in a 📦 box.
And one day who should
come along but Mr. 🦊 Fox.
"I'll catch you", said the foxie.
He opened up the lid.
But my 🐇 rabbit
    hopped into a 🕳 hole.
And there he hid.

Later, we made up this funny story
about a rabbit.

The next day, Katie said, "A robin is building a nest in our apple tree."

"I have a bird's nest," said Miss Huff. "You can see it." She put it on the science table. It was made of sticks and grass.

"I wish I could make a nest," said Jamie.

"You can," said Miss Huff. She showed us how.

First we rolled down the sides of
some lunch bags. We filled the bags
with tiny sticks and grass. Pam even
put some grass on the outside of hers.

It was fun making our nests and
putting eggs in them.

One day, Miss Huff showed us a sock-puppet and said, "A caterpillar eats and eats. It grows fat and pops its skin. Then it grows a new one. It keeps doing that. Then one day, when it is all grown up, it hangs itself up in a case called a chrysalis." She put her cater-pillar in a bag.

"In the chrysalis, it changes," she said. She reached in the bag and pulled out a. . .

"It's a butterfly," Eddie said.

"Yes," said Miss Huff. Then she told us the story of Willar Caterpillar.

Willar Caterpillar was once very small—
 but she ate all day
 and that's the way
 she grew so fat and tall.

Each time her skin-suit got too tight,
 she grew new skin that fit just right.
She slept in a chrysalis, snug and dry. . .
 and soon she grew into a butterfly.

13

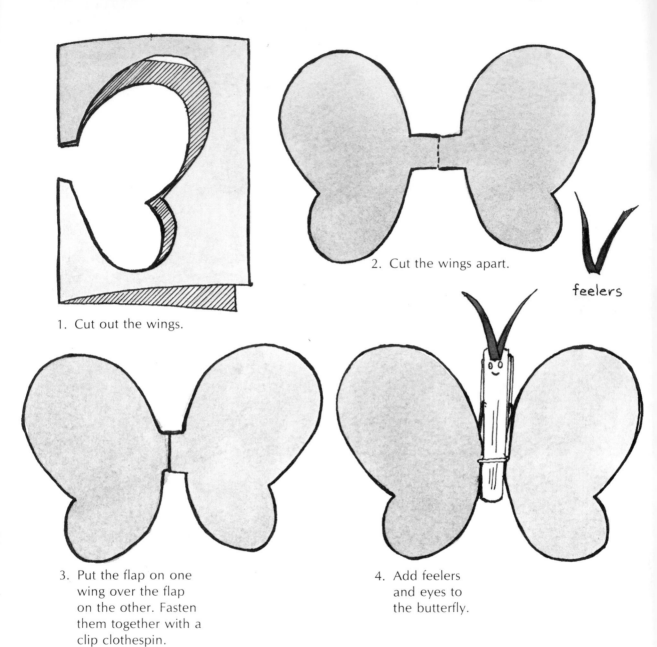

1. Cut out the wings.

2. Cut the wings apart.

feelers

3. Put the flap on one wing over the flap on the other. Fasten them together with a clip clothespin.

4. Add feelers and eyes to the butterfly.

Then we made butterflies. First we cut out paper wings. We used clothespins to put the wings together. Then we made feelers. We put them on too.

gold fish   stop light   play house

mail box   paint brush   tooth brush   butter fly

Jennifer and Katie made up a butterfly word game with some butterflies. They put two words that make another word on each pair of butterfly wings. Each pair of wings was a different color.

sail boat

Jennifer and Katie took turns mixing up the word-wings and putting them together again.

base ball

"This is fun," Katie said.

We all wanted to play so we thought up more words and made more butter-flies.

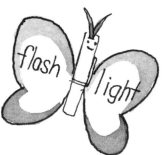

flash light

You can play this game too.

The next day, Jeff brought some polli-wogs to school. "Polliwogs are another sign of spring," said Miss Huff.

She showed us how to make a big
paper pond on the floor. We cut out
paper polliwogs and other things that
live in a pond. We put a paper clip on
each one and fished with a magnet.

Guess how many things we caught?

At storytime, Miss Huff told us this little story with a polliwog-frog puppet she had made.

One day a little polliwog
wished he could be a jumpy frog.
  *(Show polliwog, with legs hidden
  under frog and tail out.)*
In the spring, guess what he grew?
Back leg number one
and back leg number two.
  (Pull out each back leg.)
His tail became short.
And something more. . .
  (Fold tail under frog.)
He grew new front legs,
three and four.
  (Pull out front legs.)
He splashed in the water.
He sat on a log.
For he had turned into a
jumpy frog.

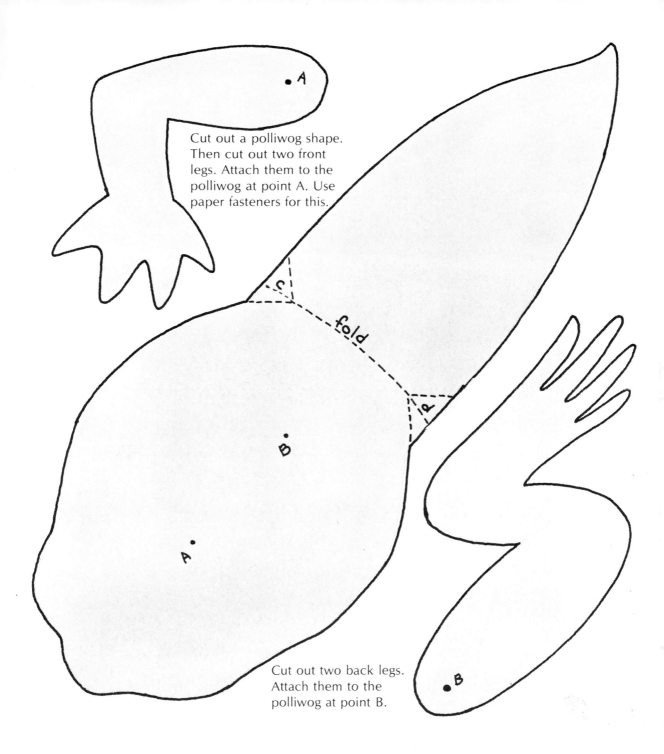

Cut out a polliwog shape.
Then cut out two front
legs. Attach them to the
polliwog at point A. Use
paper fasteners for this.

fold

Cut out two back legs.
Attach them to the
polliwog at point B.

You can make a polliwog-frog puppet and tell the story too.

After storytime, Miss Huff put a box of seeds on the work table. "Who can remember what kind of seeds we saved from Halloween?" she asked.

"Pumpkin seeds. Pumpkin seeds." Everyone remembered.

"It's a sign of spring when people start thinking of flowers and planting seeds," Miss Huff said.

We planted our pumpkin seeds. Then Miss Huff showed us the biggest seed in the world.

Guess what it was?
Guess who tasted it?

One day we made paper kites. We
made them in all kinds of spring shapes
—butterflies, frogs, flowers, even Easter
bunnies.

Then one warm, windy day. . .

we had a kite parade on the playground.
The wind pulled our kites as we ran.

One day it rained. Miss Huff said,
"It rains a lot in the spring. Rain helps
the flowers grow. Let's pretend we are
flowers."

We danced a story about flowers.
Some of us were tulip bulbs; some

were daffodils; some were Easter lilies.

Pam was the rain.

Billy was the sunshine.

Guess what? The flowers grew tall
and danced around the room.

Jennifer wanted to make flowers. So we used paper muffin cups for blossoms. And we made the centers out of yellow cotton balls. We pasted green leaves and stems on our flowers.

We folded paper plates in different ways to make baskets.

"Some Easter baskets are full of Easter eggs," said Jennifer.

"Tomorrow we will do things with eggs," Miss Huff told us.

Put a handle
on each basket.

To make a smaller
basket, fold the
paper plate twice
and staple it.

The next day, Miss Huff said, "Today we can make up Humpty-Dumpty-Easter-egg rhymes."

We made up funny rhymes. Then we made Humpty-Dumpty puppets.

Here's how we made each one:
1. We cut out two, big, paper egg shapes.
2. We wrote a rhyme on one egg shape.
3. We drew Humpty Dumpty's face on the other.
4. We put the two together, back to back.
5. Some children folded strips of paper back and forth and made arms and legs for their puppets.

Humpty Dumpty sat in a tent with an enormous elephant.

Humpty Dumpty sat on a log with a barking puppy dog.

Humpty Dumpty sat in a boat with a funny Billy goat.

Humpty Dumpty sat in a chair with a fuzzy polar bear.

Humpty Dumpty sat in a truck with a yellow quacking duck.

Here are some of our funny,
Humpty-Dumpty-Easter-egg rhymes.

29

When it came time to dye real Easter eggs, we each did two. We each had brought our own hard-boiled eggs to school.

"I will dye my eggs blue, just like a robin's eggs," said Jeff.

After the eggs were colored, Miss Huff showed us how to make Easter baskets from empty milk cartons. We decorated our baskets to take home.

Before we went home, we made
Easter-bunny hats.

Miss Huff painted whiskers on us,
and we hopped home!